101 Things Children Can Do To Annoy Their Parents

C0-AVC-756

Cover by Erik Hollander
assisted by *The Ideas Network.*

Illustrations by
Richard Gunther

Ray Comfort's

101 Things Children Can Do To Annoy Their Parents

Bridge-Logos *Publishers*
North Brunswick, NJ

101 Things Children Can Do To Annoy Their Parents

Copyright©1998 by Ray Comfort
International Standard Book Number: 0-88270-759-0
Library of Congress Catalog Card Number: 98-73143

Published by:
Bridge-Logos *Publishers*
1300 Airport Road, Suite E
North Brunswick, NJ 08902

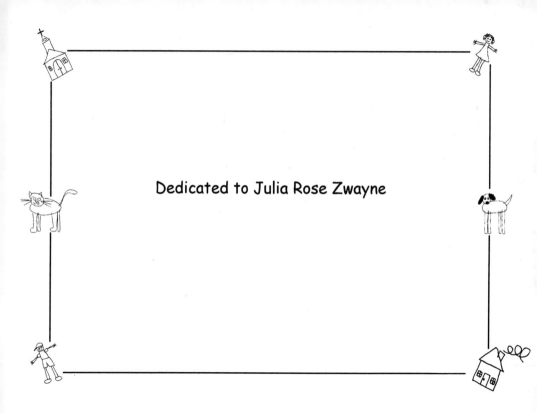

Dedicated to Julia Rose Zwayne

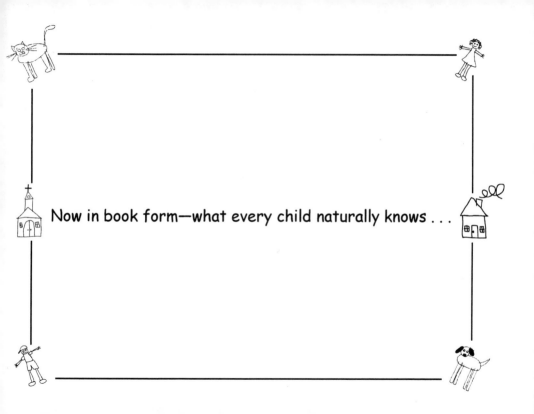

Now in book form—what every child naturally knows . . .

1. Wait until your parents are on the phone before you whine.

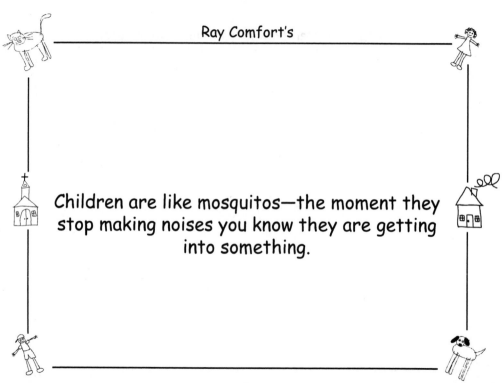

Children are like mosquitos—the moment they stop making noises you know they are getting into something.

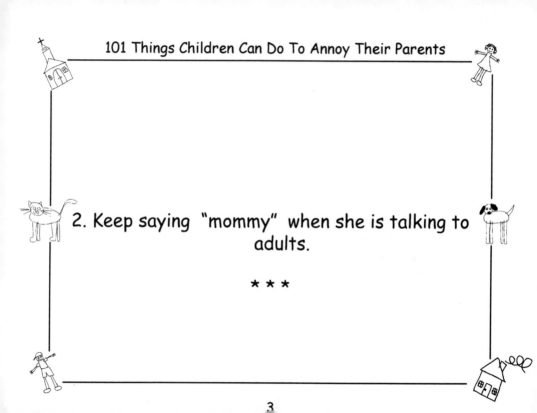

2. Keep saying "mommy" when she is talking to adults.

* * *

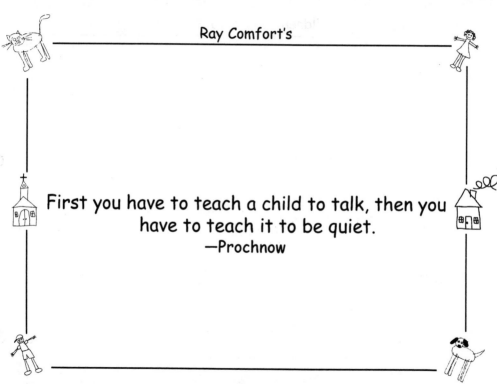

First you have to teach a child to talk, then you have to teach it to be quiet.
—Prochnow

Dad . . . Dad!

Kids seem to always want to talk when you're speaking with another adult. This was the case with my daughter when she was about seven years old. I was outside talking with three or four young men, when Rachel grabbed my hand and quietly said, "Dad . . ." What I was saying was important, so I ignored her. Once again I heard, "Dad . . ." and once again I ignored her. A third time I heard "Dad . . . ," instead of ignoring her, I put my fatherly hand on her warm little head and gently rubbed it to let her know that I was aware of her, and that I would get to her in time.

It was then I discovered why she had been saying "Dad." A bird dropping had landed on her head.

3. Throw your bottle on the floor and see how much fluff will stick to the nipple.

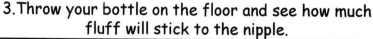

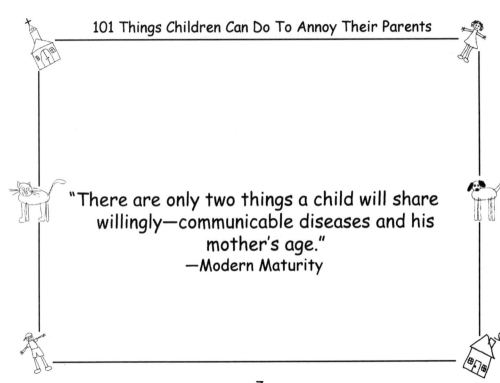

"There are only two things a child will share willingly—communicable diseases and his mother's age."
—Modern Maturity

4. Put dirty or sticky hands on clean windows.

* * *

5. Pull a handful of fur out of the dog. Put the fur into your mouth.

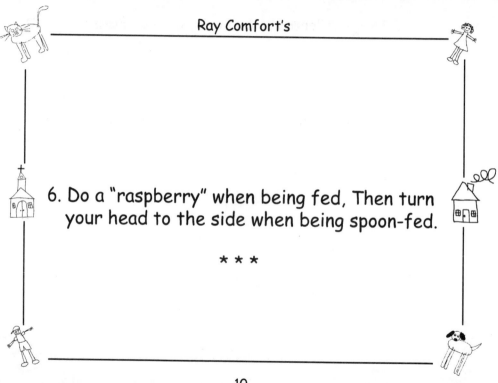

6. Do a "raspberry" when being fed, Then turn your head to the side when being spoon-fed.

* * *

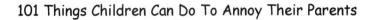

Distasteful

We took our three kids out to a meal at a friend's place. This was risky because our youngest hated everything that humanity ate, except bread. So before the meal was served, we told our friends that he preferred just to chew on a piece of bread. This saved the embarassment of telling the hostess that she didn't like her cooking.

However, our oldest (then six years old) looked at the food set before him and said in a nice, clear voice, "Yuk! I don't like this. When are we going home?"

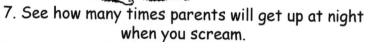

7. See how many times parents will get up at night when you scream.

How to Make a Monster

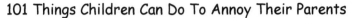

We never appreciated silence until we had kids. Now, when we hear it, we stop and listen. Children taught us a lot. We now look back and see that we made the mistake of feeding one of our kids every time she screamed as a baby. It wasn't long before we created a cookie monster, who was as wide as she was high.

The monster developed a scream as loud as a 747 at full throttle. Knowing that god had graciously made the noise exit the food entry to give us a little peace, we decided to put a pacifier in the mouth. that gave us three nights of unbroken sleep. Unbroken, that is, until we heard a "ping" noise that would become very familiar. It took three nights of sucking for her to realize that there was no taste bud material in the pacifier, so she spat it out with gusto, and put the jet

13

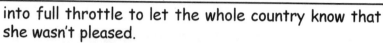

into full throttle to let the whole country know that she wasn't pleased.

Some kind person told us to dip the pacifier in honey. That worked . . . for a night. We became very familiar with a pre-sucking noise that built up to a loud "ping," as she gained more expertise in the exercise. Then there was the five seconds of silence as the lungs of the 747 pulled in oxygen, before letting out the scream that the neighborhood must have by that time also become familiar with.

Sue and I took turns at sleepwalking into her room. We would keep the light off so that we didn't wake up. I would keep my eyes closed and just follow the noise in the room. Doing this exercise 6-8 times each night, I knew where the pacifier would land. I would kneel down in the dark and find it with my hand. Next was the pulling of carpet fluff off the wet and sticky

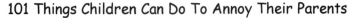

pacifier. I would make my way to the crib, and feel for the dish of honey. Where was it? . . . oh. There it is . . . (as I pulled my fingers out of the sticky honey). Pacifier into the honey, and into the screaming baby's . . . cheek. Where is that mouth? Ah. Silence . . . for a while. The morning light would reveal a face that looked like a well-used honey jar.

The eight times a night aerobics lasted for about three months. We ended up zombies, and the baby ended up with cavities in her front teeth.

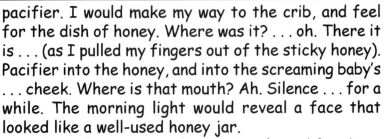

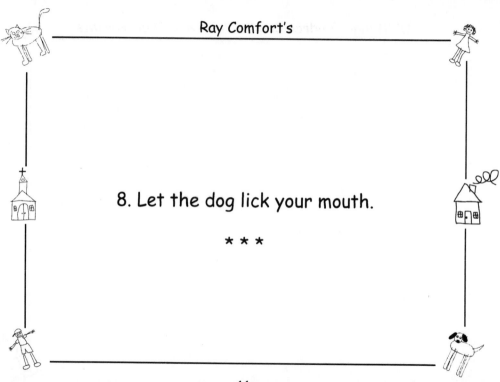

8. Let the dog lick your mouth.

* * *

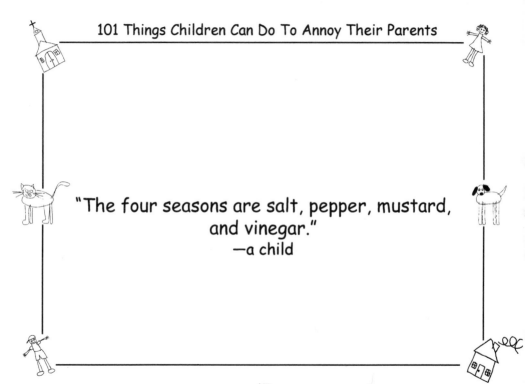

"The four seasons are salt, pepper, mustard,
and vinegar."
—a child

9. Don't cry until your parents are soundly asleep.

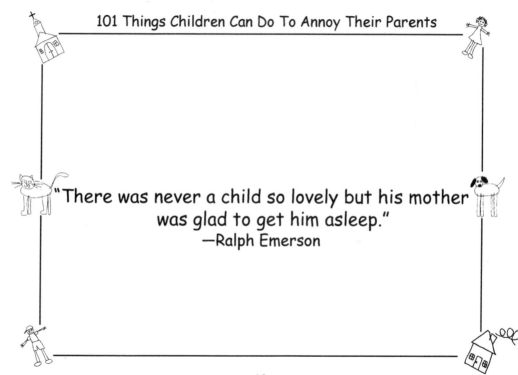

"There was never a child so lovely but his mother
was glad to get him asleep."
—Ralph Emerson

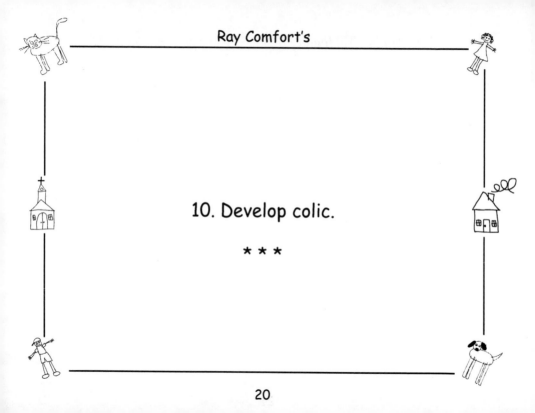

10. Develop colic.

* * *

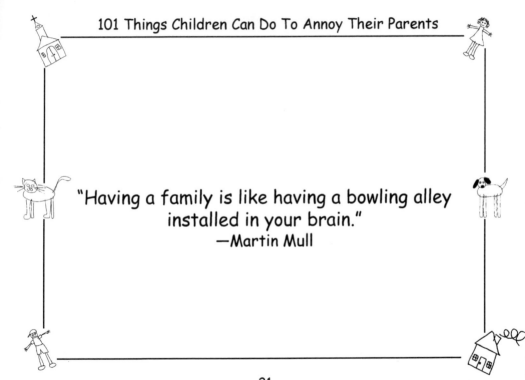

"Having a family is like having a bowling alley
installed in your brain."
—Martin Mull

11. Take candy out of your mouth, handle it, then touch parent's clothes.

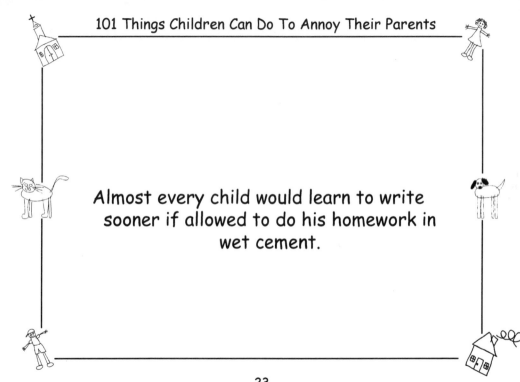

Almost every child would learn to write sooner if allowed to do his homework in wet cement.

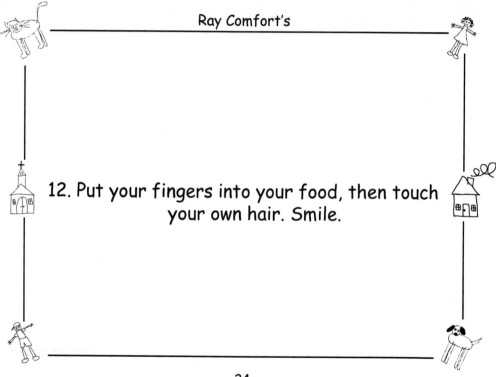

12. Put your fingers into your food, then touch your own hair. Smile.

13. No matter how wide the back seat is in the car, fight with your brother or sister over who sits where.

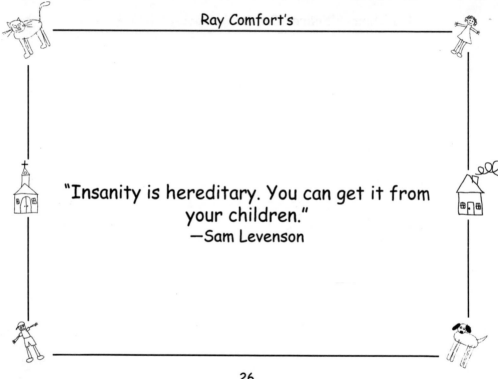

"Insanity is hereditary. You can get it from
your children."
—Sam Levenson

Exhausted

Our kids used to spend hours playing in my car as it sat in the garage. I had the keys in the house, what harm could be done? Plenty. They managed to push it out of the garage while the car door was open. As it went out, the door caught on the garage and buckled itself and the side of the car. This was around the time the two eldest for some reason talked the youngest into wrapping his lips around the exhaust pipe.

I guess he was trying to blow up my car.

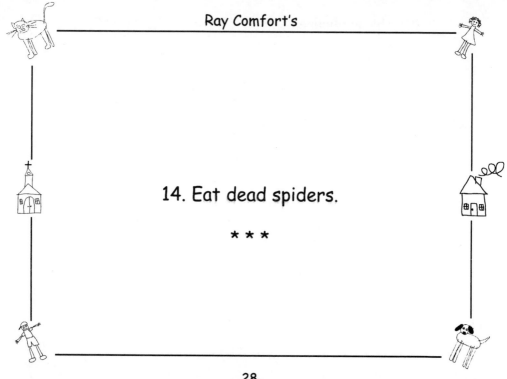

14. Eat dead spiders.

* * *

15. Eat flies.

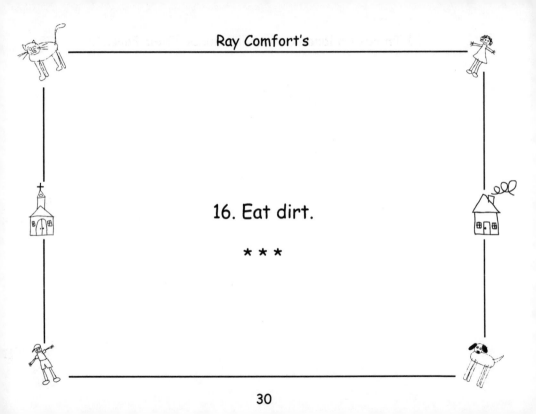

16. Eat dirt.

* * *

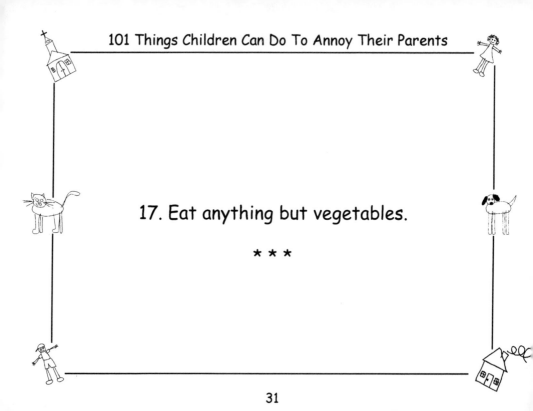

17. Eat anything but vegetables.

* * *

Getting Around

A parent tries to keep a child happy. This is for the sake of the parent as much as for the sake of the child. Sometimes however, it isn't possible. My four-year-old pointed to where he wanted me to put ketchup on his plate. I carefully put it exactly where he had pointed, but to my surprise, he let out a scream and went into hysterics. What was my offense?

The ketchup hadn't made a perfect circle.

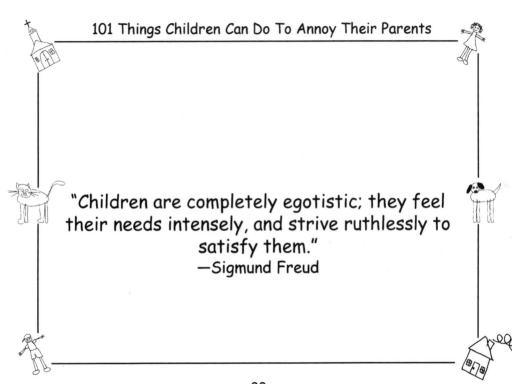

"Children are completely egotistic; they feel their needs intensely, and strive ruthlessly to satisfy them."
—Sigmund Freud

18. Learn to wriggle out of your car seat.

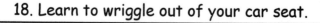

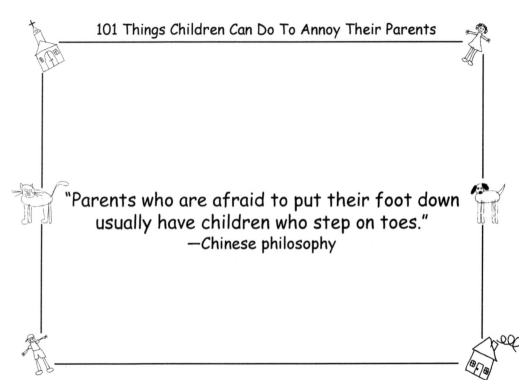

"Parents who are afraid to put their foot down
usually have children who step on toes."
—Chinese philosophy

19. Crawl towards water.

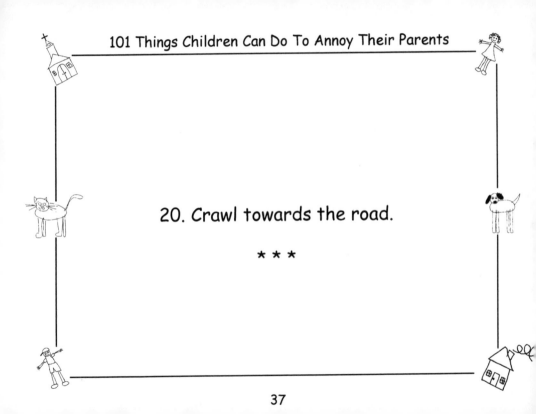

20. Crawl towards the road.

* * *

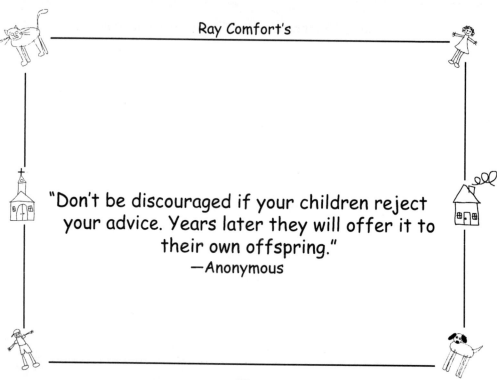

"Don't be discouraged if your children reject your advice. Years later they will offer it to their own offspring."
—Anonymous

21. Run towards cliffs.

No Turning Back

I decided to follow my son as he rode his new bike. I carefully instructed him about the road rules. I taught him how to put his hand up when stopping, and to put his hand out when turning, to let the driver know what his intentions were. A good father . . . that's what I am.

The big moment came when I let him onto the road. Seven-years-old is young but he is a sensible lad. I watched as his hand went out exactly as I taught him. He was letting me know that he was about to turn in front of my car, as I drove slowly behind him. Then he turned . . . without looking behind him!

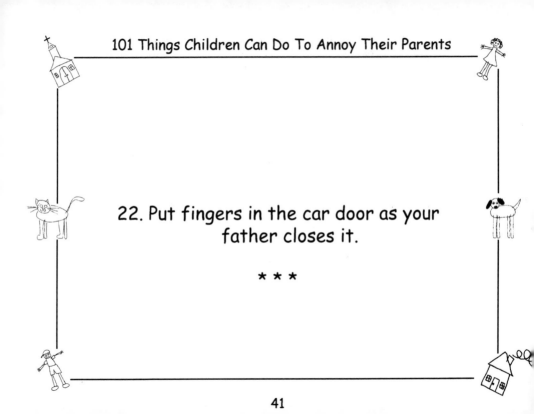

22. Put fingers in the car door as your
father closes it.

* * *

23. If you are on a plane, scream for the whole flight.

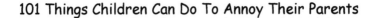

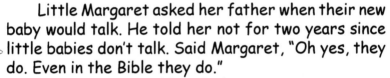

Little Margaret asked her father when their new baby would talk. He told her not for two years since little babies don't talk. Said Margaret, "Oh yes, they do. Even in the Bible they do."

"Who did?" asked her father.

She replied, "Sister read the Bible to us this morning and I heard with my own ears that Job cursed the day he was born."

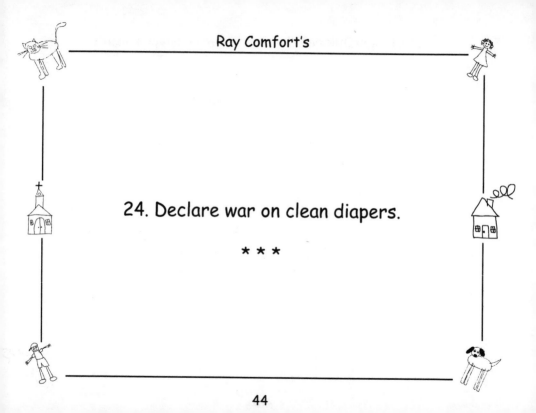

24. Declare war on clean diapers.

* * *

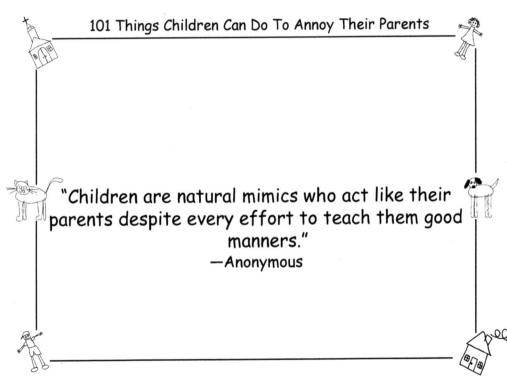

"Children are natural mimics who act like their parents despite every effort to teach them good manners."
—Anonymous

25. Suck old blankets.

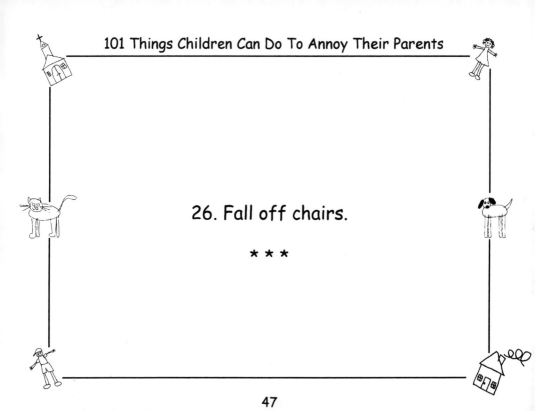

26. Fall off chairs.

* * *

27. Hate your bath.
Eat the soap.

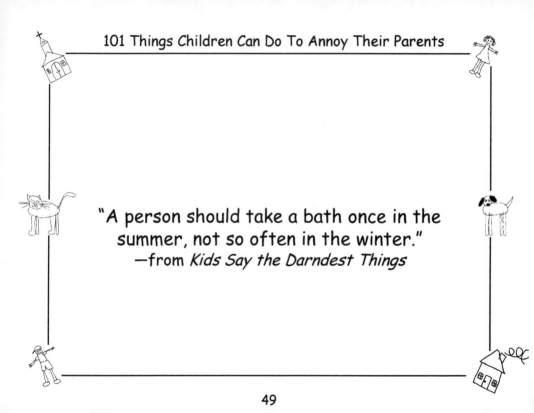

"A person should take a bath once in the
summer, not so often in the winter."
—from *Kids Say the Darndest Things*

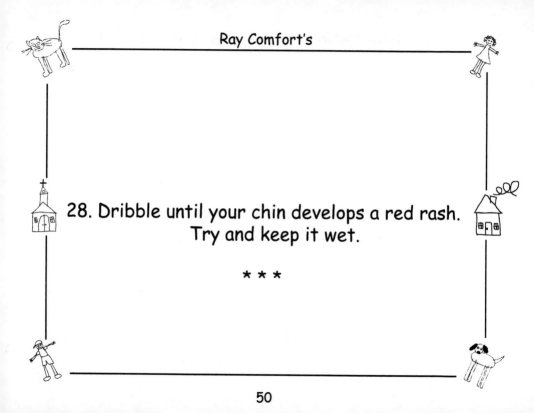

28. Dribble until your chin develops a red rash. Try and keep it wet.

* * *

29. Hate having your face washed.

Seeing Red

A small girl was standing quietly as her mother and the lady next door talked. Suddenly she asked the neighbor if she could see her newly painted bathroom. The neighbor was delighted.

As they entered the bathroom the child turned to her mother and said, "Mommy, the color doesn't make me sick."

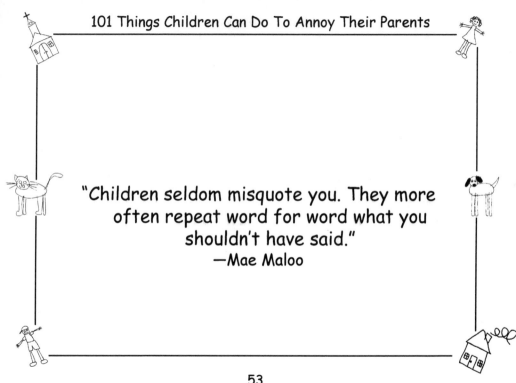

"Children seldom misquote you. They more often repeat word for word what you shouldn't have said."
—Mae Maloo

30. Pull the hair of other kids.

* * *

31. Grab the cat's whiskers. Pull them out.

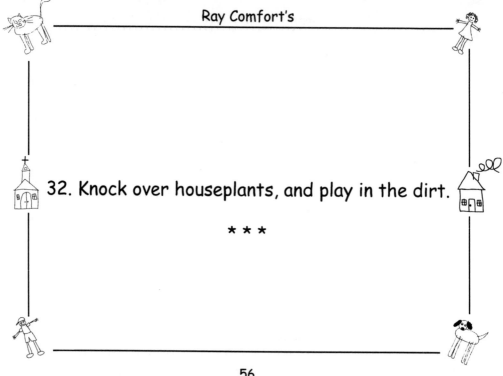

32. Knock over houseplants, and play in the dirt.

* * *

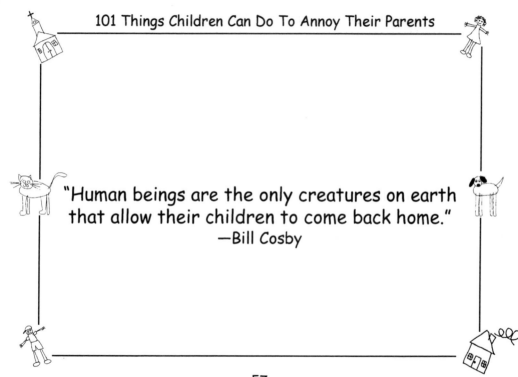

"Human beings are the only creatures on earth that allow their children to come back home."
—Bill Cosby

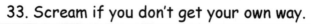
33. Scream if you don't get your own way.

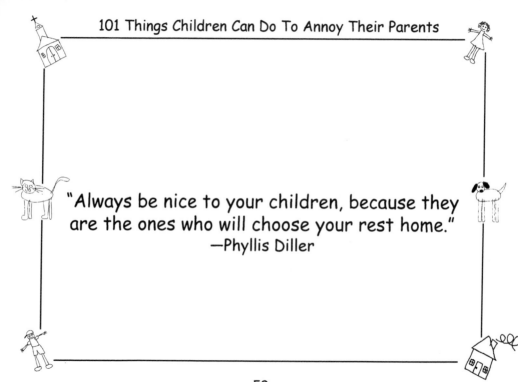

"Always be nice to your children, because they are the ones who will choose your rest home."
—Phyllis Diller

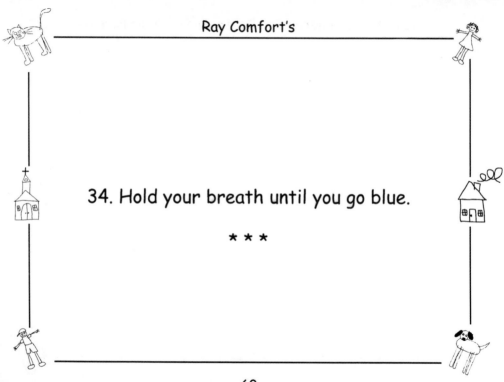

34. Hold your breath until you go blue.

* * *

"The parts of speech are lungs and air."
—a child

35. Knock over lamp shades, or anything that can break.

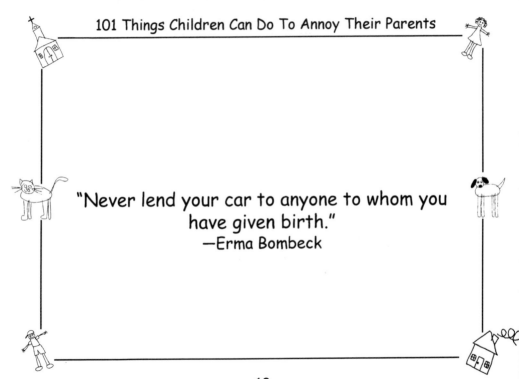

"Never lend your car to anyone to whom you have given birth."
—Erma Bombeck

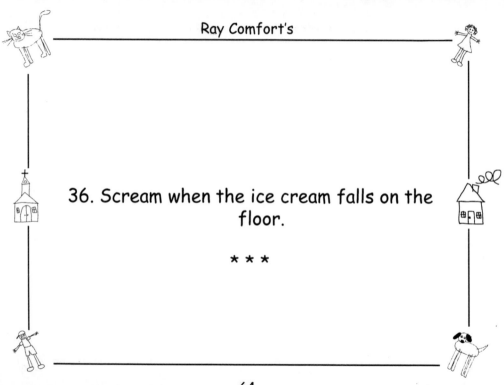

36. Scream when the ice cream falls on the floor.

* * *

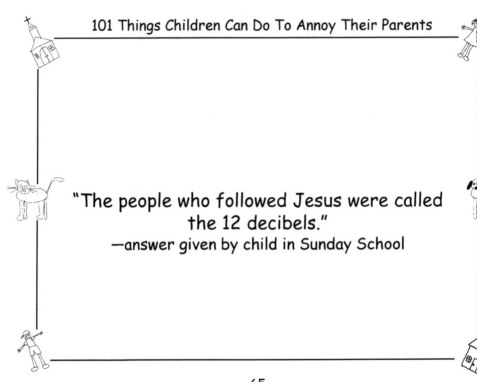

"The people who followed Jesus were called
the 12 decibels."
—answer given by child in Sunday School

37. Look for opportunities to wander off.

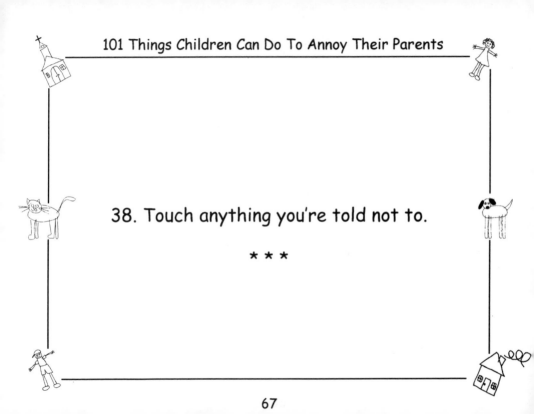

38. Touch anything you're told not to.

* * *

39. Get hold of a pen and get the ink on your new clothes.

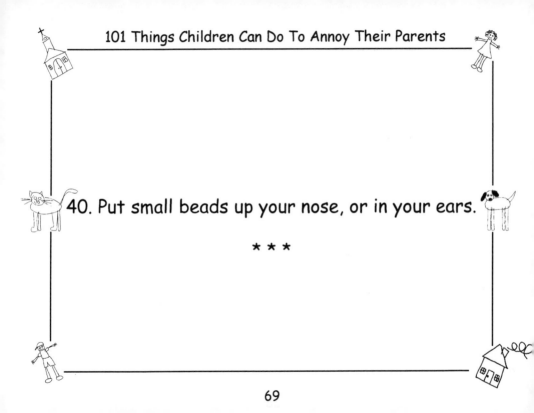

40. Put small beads up your nose, or in your ears.

* * *

We Know

We have three children . . . one of each. They used to be little but we made the mistake of feeding them.

Life is strange. You meet the girl of your dreams, fall in love, get married, and have a child. The kid lives in the refrigerator. Suddenly there's a huge pair of hairy legs sitting in your favorite chair. He won't get off, and he laughs when you ask him for the remote control.

41. Lose one of your shoes.

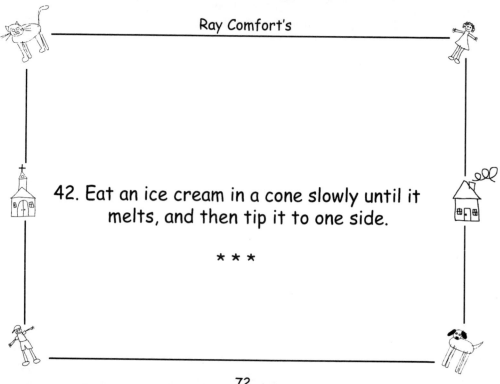

42. Eat an ice cream in a cone slowly until it melts, and then tip it to one side.

* * *

"The climate is hottest next to the Creator."
—a child

43. Hate having your hair washed.

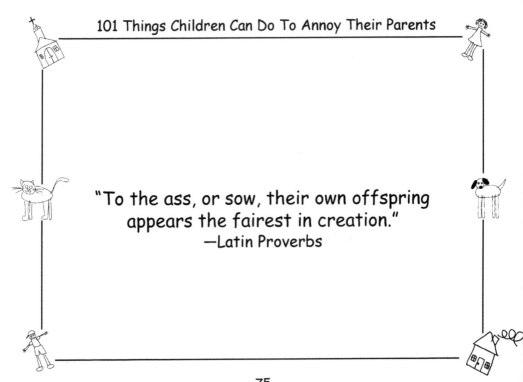

"To the ass, or sow, their own offspring
appears the fairest in creation."
—Latin Proverbs

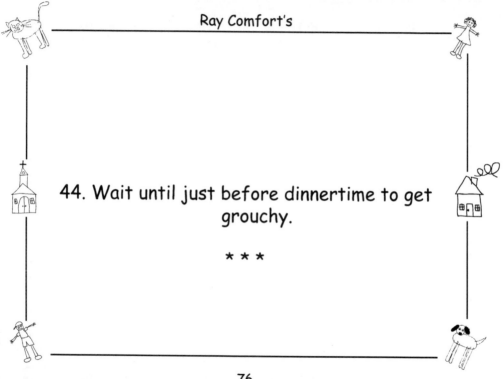

44. Wait until just before dinnertime to get grouchy.

* * *

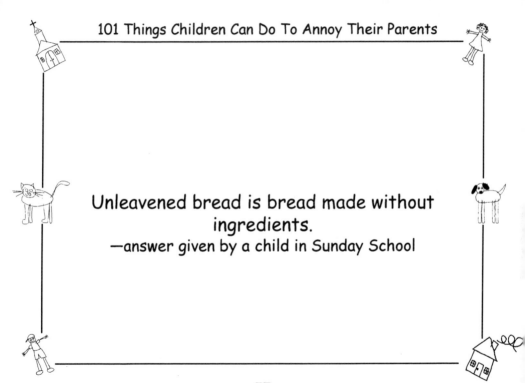

Unleavened bread is bread made without ingredients.
—answer given by a child in Sunday School

45. When holding anything that can spill, disregard gravity.

"A horse divided against itself cannot stand."
—from *Student Bloopers*

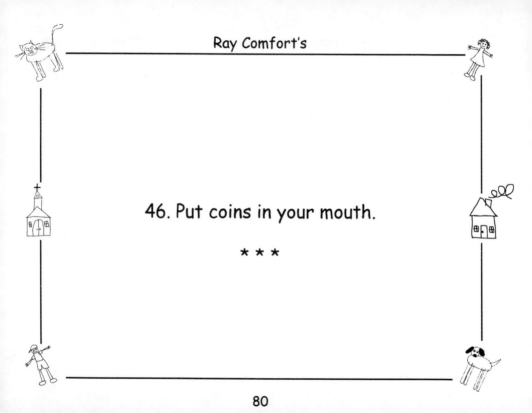

46. Put coins in your mouth.

* * *

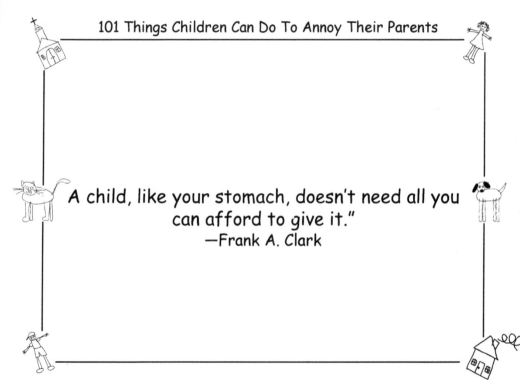

A child, like your stomach, doesn't need all you
can afford to give it."
—Frank A. Clark

47. Pull on tablecloths at dinnertime.

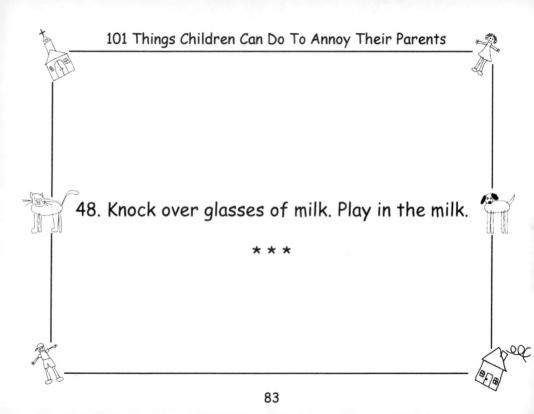

48. Knock over glasses of milk. Play in the milk.

* * *

May We See You A Moment, Outside?

Man has figured out a lot of ways of making himself miserable, but the soundest idea he has hit on in a long while is to take a small child into a public restaurant.

A child psychologist, whose name we will not reveal because of a genuine concern for his safety, now comes forward with the suggestion that the child should be given what's known as an object lesson. This involves taking a child to a restaurant and doing all the things a child does. We can understand how this would be gratifying to the child, but we shudder to think of the effect on the other customers. For example:

1. Knock the milk over, yourself. To beat the child to it you will have to strike with the speed of a cobra. Try to hit the glass in such a way that the milk flows across the table and into the lap of an adult. You will probably never achieve the casual, sure touch that the child displays,

but you can do a good workmanlike job if you apply yourself spiritedly.

2. Kick the table so as to spill coffee into the saucers. A well-placed kick during the soup course can get the entire party moved to another table.

3. Twist around in your chair until, as nearly as possible, you have your back to the table. This permits you to see the coming and going of the waiters, the seating of customers, and makes it possible to ignore the food completely.

4. Most of the food, of course, goes on the floor where it belongs, but a certain amount should be saved for the tablecloth. Spear the lamb chop violently and let the fork strike the plate a glancing blow. This propels the peas across the table, which is better theatre than having them dribble over the sides of the plate.

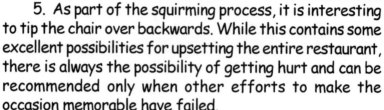

5. As part of the squirming process, it is interesting to tip the chair over backwards. While this contains some excellent possibilities for upsetting the entire restaurant, there is always the possibility of getting hurt and can be recommended only when other efforts to make the occasion memorable have failed.

6. It's good social custom to get down from the chair and wander around other tables, staring at strangers and even inquiring what they are eating. This adds immeasurably to the sociability of the meal.

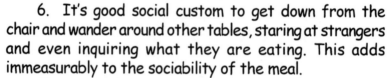

These are the main points to remember in teaching the child a lesson, but there's one other thing. Keep your eye on the manager and be ready to leave as soon as you see him make a furtive telephone call from the cashier's desk. If there's a side door, take it.

—Caskie Stinnett

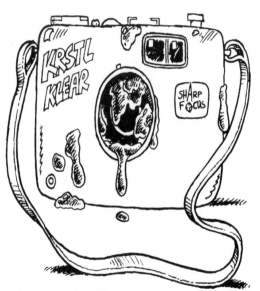

49. Put sticky fingers on camera lens.

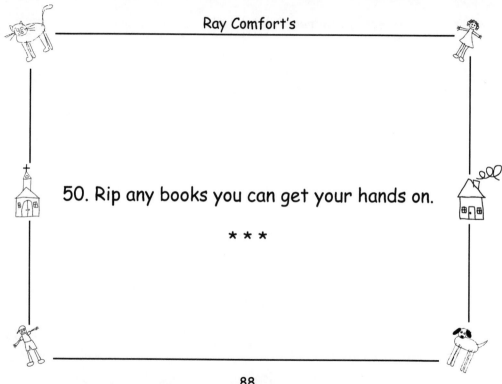

50. Rip any books you can get your hands on.

* * *

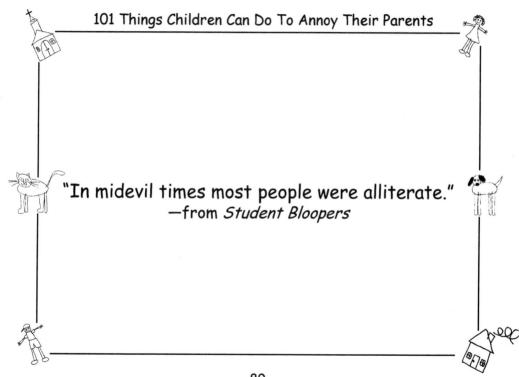

"In midevil times most people were alliterate."
—from *Student Bloopers*

51. Push volume button on television.

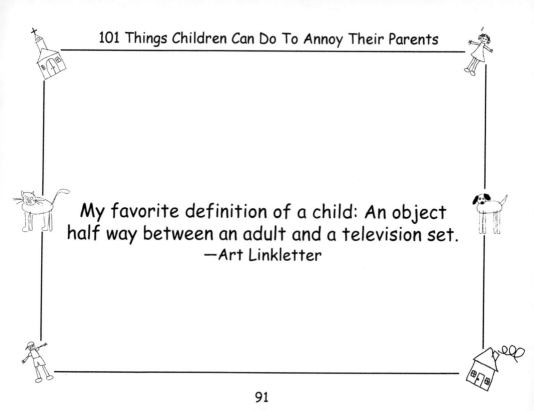

My favorite definition of a child: An object
half way between an adult and a television set.
—Art Linkletter

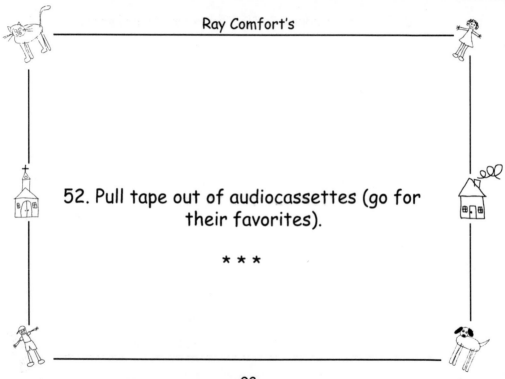

52. Pull tape out of audiocassettes (go for their favorites).

* * *

53. Pull tape out of videocassettes.

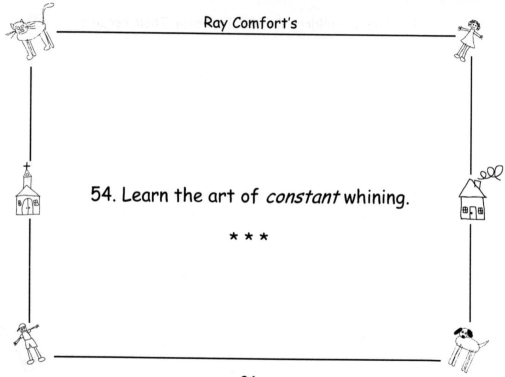

54. Learn the art of *constant* whining.

* * *

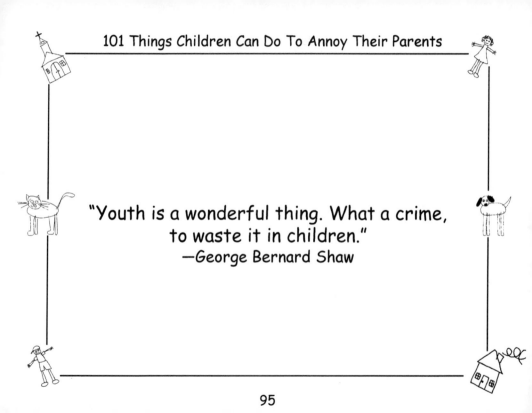

"Youth is a wonderful thing. What a crime,
to waste it in children."
—George Bernard Shaw

55. Learn how to do the "brat back-arch" when sitting on their knees.

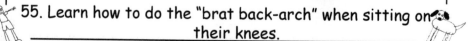

56. When told "No!" keep on asking anyway.

* * *

57. Eat out of the dog's dish.

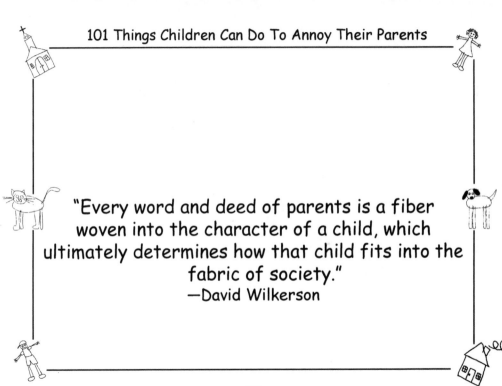

"Every word and deed of parents is a fiber woven into the character of a child, which ultimately determines how that child fits into the fabric of society."
—David Wilkerson

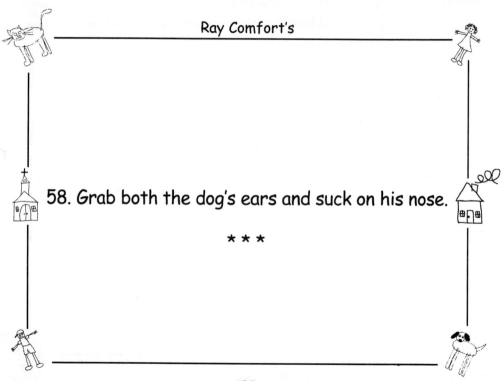

58. Grab both the dog's ears and suck on his nose.

* * *

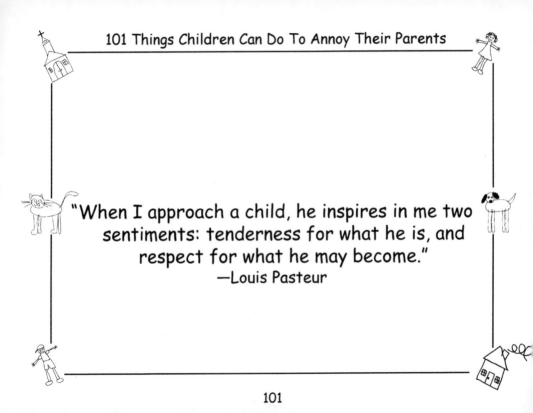

"When I approach a child, he inspires in me two sentiments: tenderness for what he is, and respect for what he may become."
—Louis Pasteur

59. Pull the dog's tail until he growls.

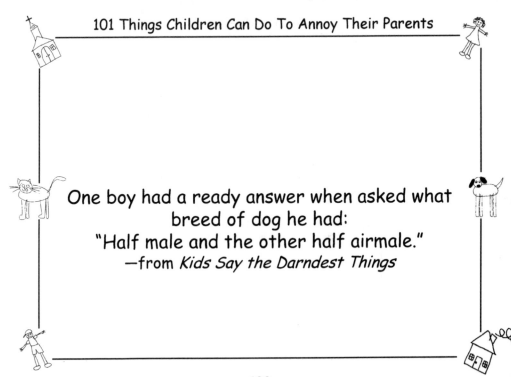

One boy had a ready answer when asked what breed of dog he had:
"Half male and the other half airmale."
—from *Kids Say the Darndest Things*

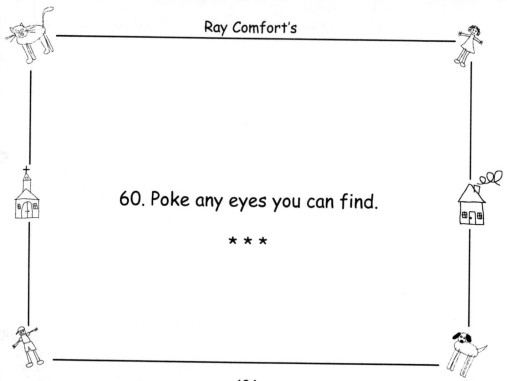

60. Poke any eyes you can find.

* * *

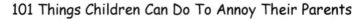

What are you learning at school that you can tell us about?

They teach you not to fight with your friends.

How do they do that?

They read from the Bible, where Jesus says, "Thou shalt not kill."

I'm happy to learn that they've stopped the killing on the playgrounds this way. But tell me, have you been punished lately?

Yes.

What for?

Hitting a kid in the face with a cupcake.

Why did you do that?

It's not in the Bible.

—From *Kids Say the Darndest Things*

61. Get under parent's feet to try and trip them; especially during meal preparation.

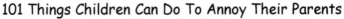

What Makes Children Laugh?

I'd like to know what goes on inside my youngest daughter when she decides to get funny in a letter. She'll spend half an hour absorbed in writing to a great aunt in Elmira. When she's finished, she brings the letter in to us and reads:

"Dear Aunt Florence: Last night Daddy fell over a duck."

My wife and I look at one another with puzzled frowns. My wife says, "What on earth do you want to say a thing like that for?"

"To make my letter funny," Mary says.

"Well, it's silly," my wife says. "I think you should change it."

Mary studies it thoughtfully. She suddenly puts her head on her arm, disappears behind her hair, wraps her legs around the chair, erases about half an ounce of paper off the page, and starts over, as if carving her initials in the table.

She looks up and says, "I wrote something else."

"Well, that's better," my wife says. "What did you write?"

"Last night Daddy fell over a kangaroo," Mary reads.

She'll keep this up until somebody stops her and makes her write, "I am saving stamps." But the point is, she's not the least embarassed that her jokes are flopping like cool Yorkshire puddings. She's completely cold-blooded about the whole thing.

—Robert Thomas Allen

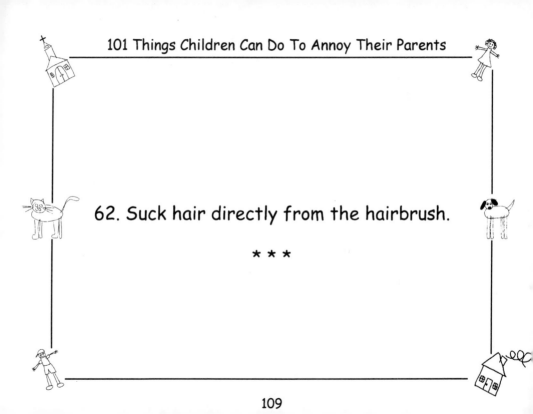

62. Suck hair directly from the hairbrush.

* * *

63. Eat some more out of the dog's dish.

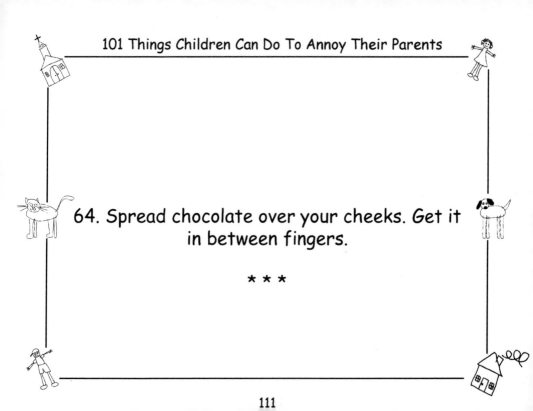

64. Spread chocolate over your cheeks. Get it in between fingers.

* * *

65. Get fingers sticky, then touch parent's glasses.

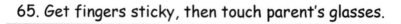

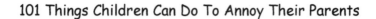

The Abandon Child Law

It is illegal in forty-seven states to leave a child in a rest room and pretend it was a mistake. Maryland and Utah are sympathetic to parents if they can produce a doctor's certificate showing a mental deterioration caused by the trip. Alaska (which is quite permissive) allows a mild sedation for the children.

—Erma Bombeck

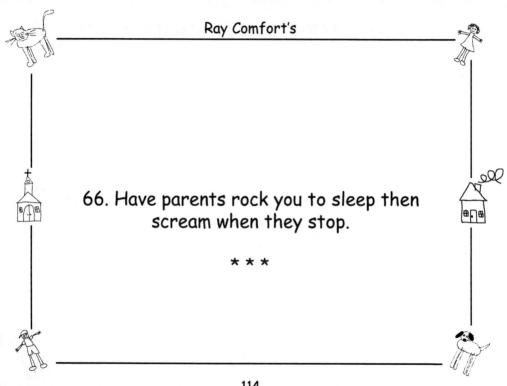

66. Have parents rock you to sleep then scream when they stop.

* * *

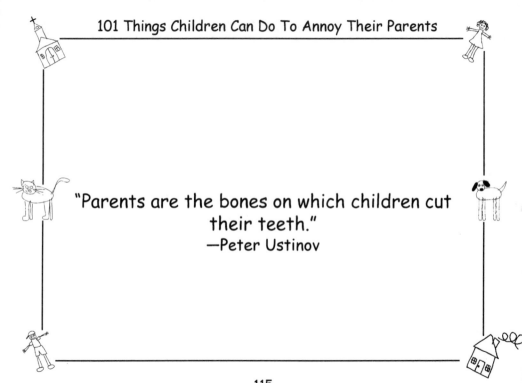

"Parents are the bones on which children cut their teeth."
—Peter Ustinov

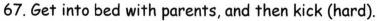

67. Get into bed with parents, and then kick (hard).

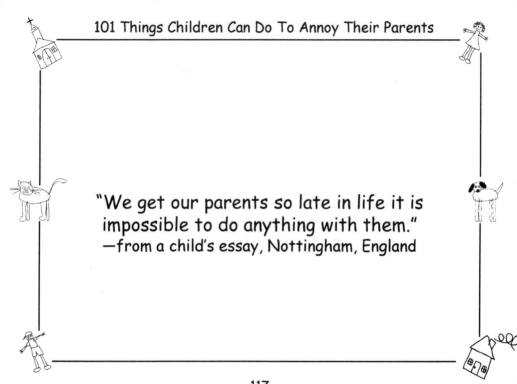

"We get our parents so late in life it is impossible to do anything with them."
—from a child's essay, Nottingham, England

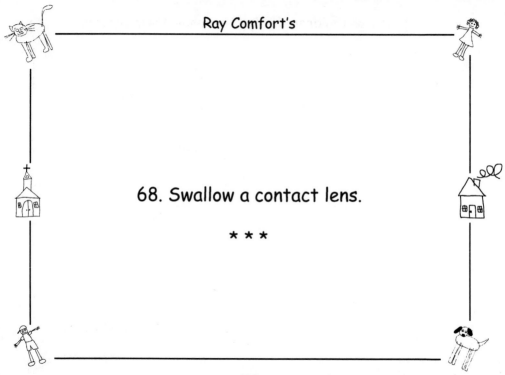

68. Swallow a contact lens.

* * *

69. Constantly hit a food-filled spoon on your plate during a meal.

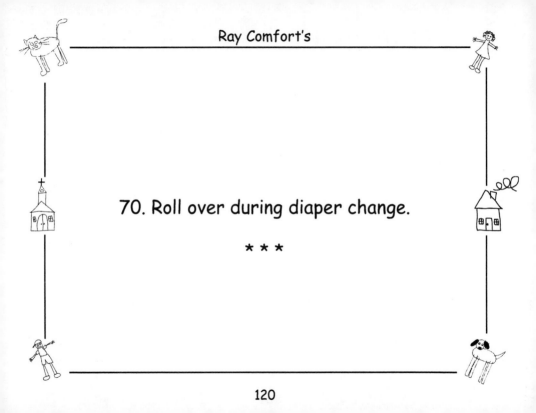

70. Roll over during diaper change.

* * *

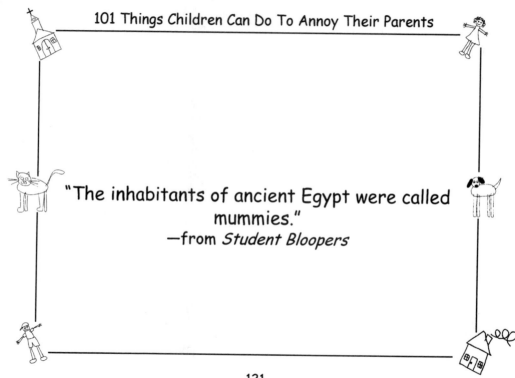

"The inhabitants of ancient Egypt were called
mummies."
—from *Student Bloopers*

71. Resist being dressed.

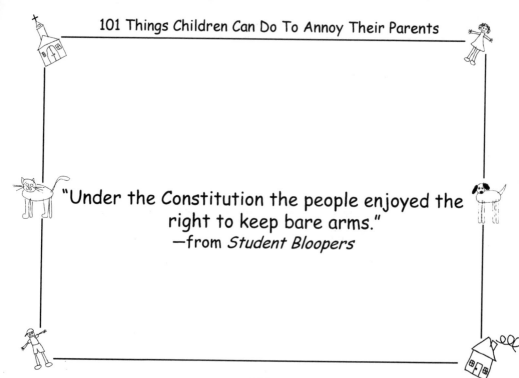

"Under the Constitution the people enjoyed the right to keep bare arms."
—from *Student Bloopers*

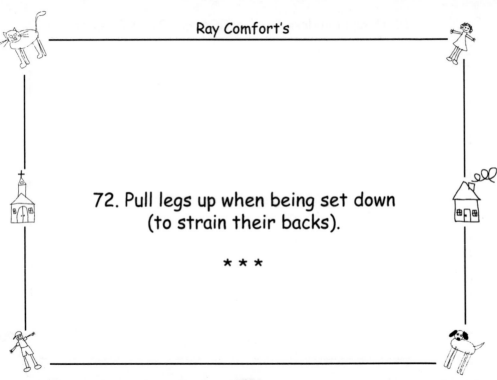

72. Pull legs up when being set down
(to strain their backs).

* * *

73. Hold onto blankets or sheets when being lifted out of bed (to strain backs).

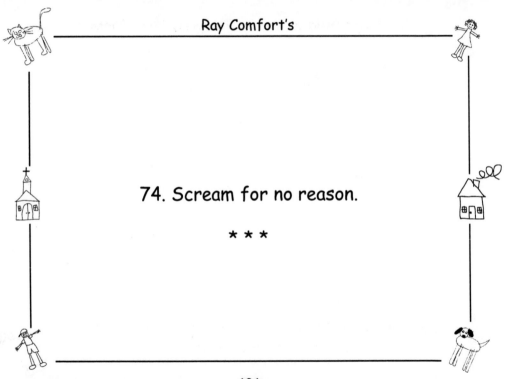

74. Scream for no reason.

* * *

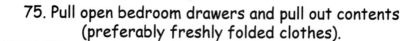

75. Pull open bedroom drawers and pull out contents (preferably freshly folded clothes).

76. Get soap on your hands and rub your eyes.
Then scream.

* * *

77. Feed your food to the dog and let him lick your hands.

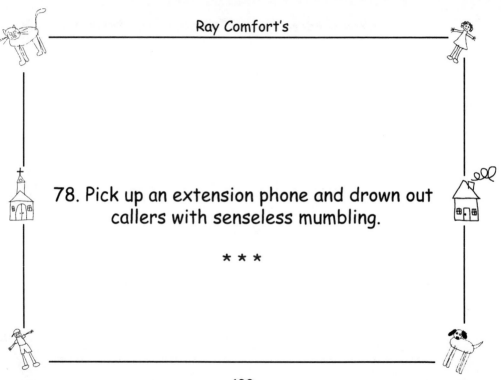

78. Pick up an extension phone and drown out callers with senseless mumbling.

* * *

"One of their children, Cain, once asked,
'Am I my brother's son?'"
—from *Student Bloopers*

79. Put ink end of a ballpoint pen in your mouth, then suck.

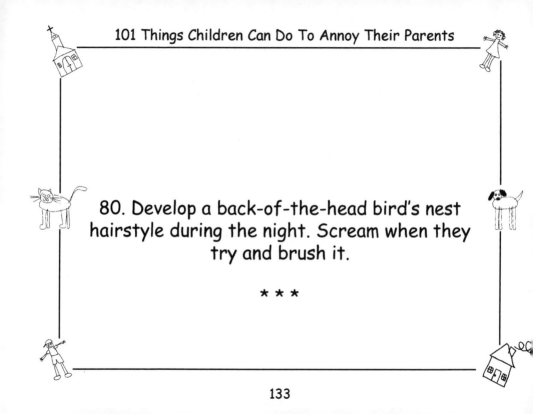

80. Develop a back-of-the-head bird's nest hairstyle during the night. Scream when they try and brush it.

* * *

81. Squeeze the cat until its eyes bulge.

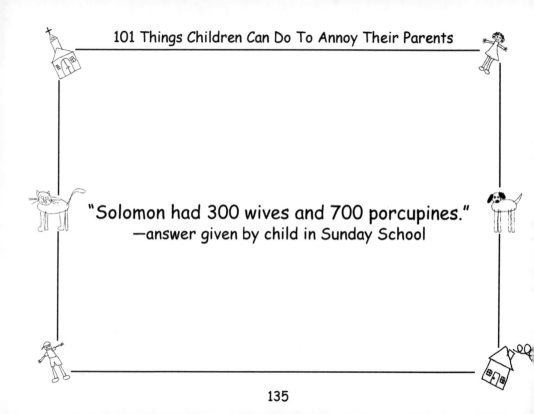

"Solomon had 300 wives and 700 porcupines."
—answer given by child in Sunday School

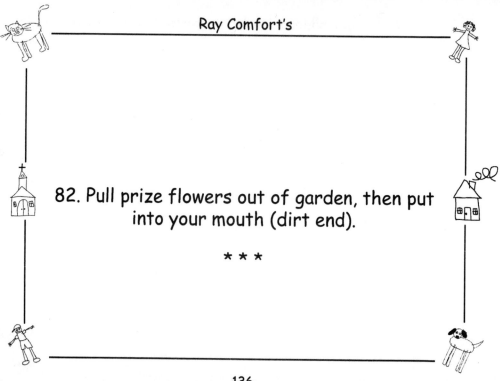

82. Pull prize flowers out of garden, then put into your mouth (dirt end).

* * *

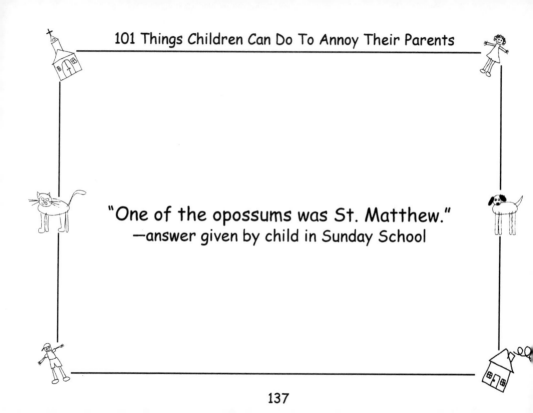

"One of the opossums was St. Matthew."
—answer given by child in Sunday School

83. Grab anything heavy when being picked up.

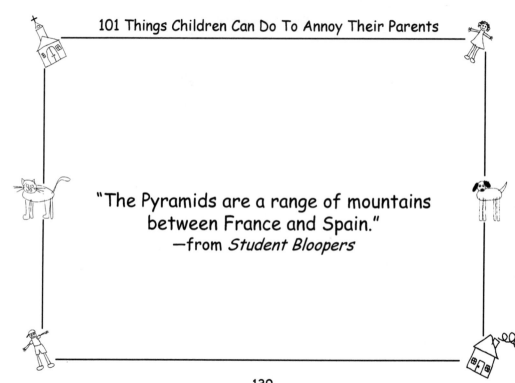

"The Pyramids are a range of mountains
between France and Spain."
—from *Student Bloopers*

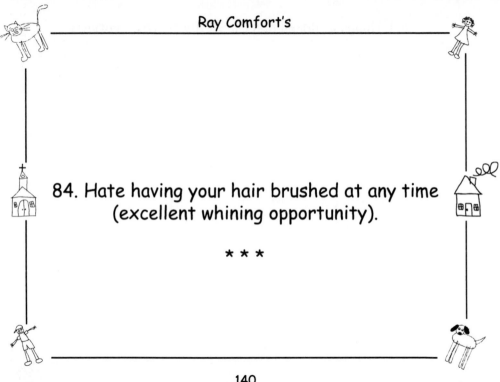

84. Hate having your hair brushed at any time (excellent whining opportunity).

* * *

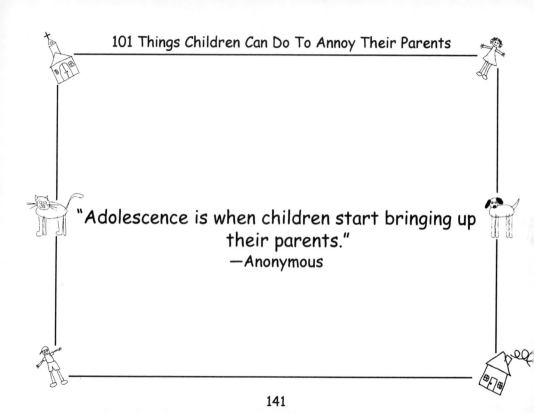

"Adolescence is when children start bringing up their parents."
—Anonymous

85. Draw on walls with crayons.

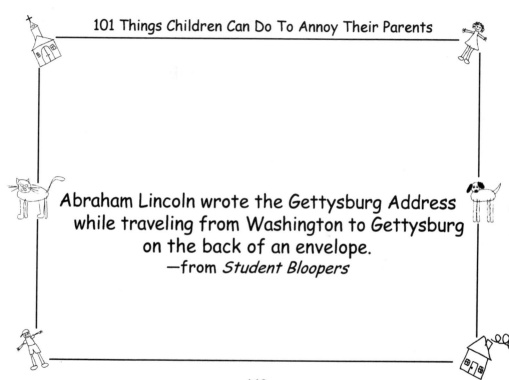

Abraham Lincoln wrote the Gettysburg Address
while traveling from Washington to Gettysburg
on the back of an envelope.
—from *Student Bloopers*

86. Let the bird out of the cage (when the cat is in the room).

* * *

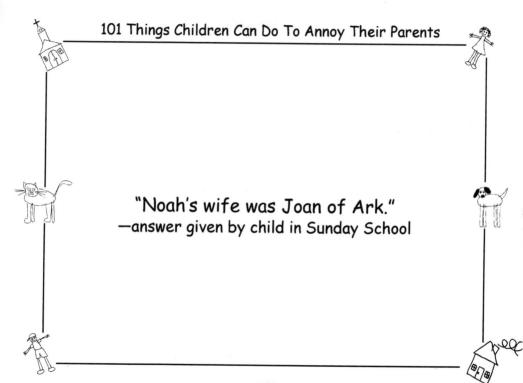

"Noah's wife was Joan of Ark."
—answer given by child in Sunday School

87. Unravel the whole roll of toilet paper.

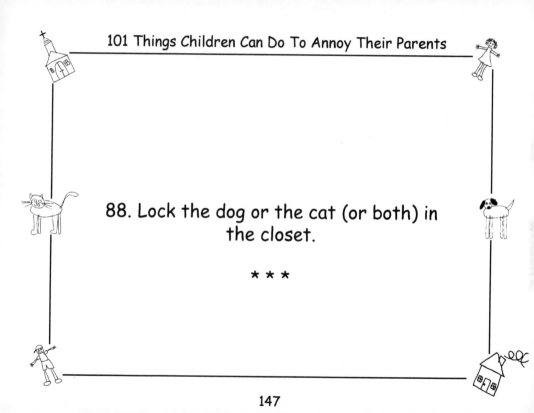

88. Lock the dog or the cat (or both) in the closet.

* * *

89. Pull over the toy box.

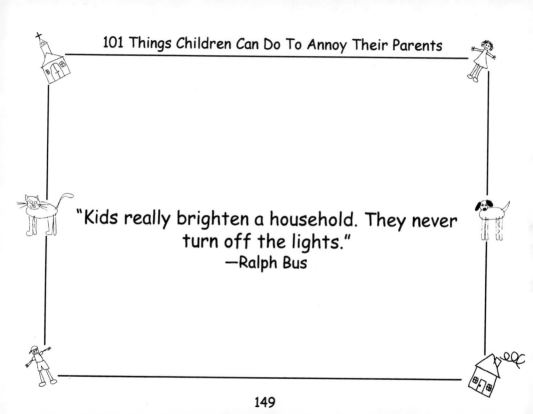

"Kids really brighten a household. They never turn off the lights."
—Ralph Bus

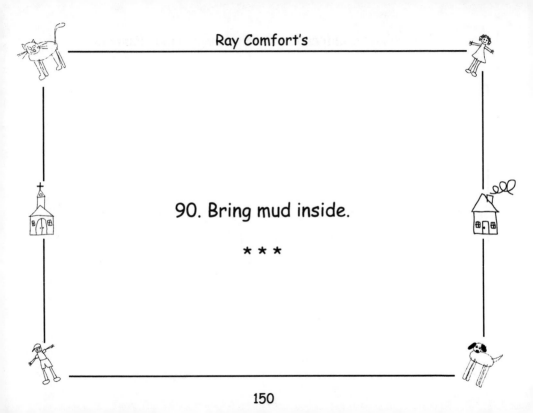

90. Bring mud inside.

* * *

Father, report card in hand: "Son, it's too bad they don't give a grade for courage. You would get an 'A' for bringing this report card home."

91. Get into the kitchen trash bin. Eat.

Impressed

Kids often imitate their parents. A friend of mine boasted to his son, how, when he was a teenager, he had a truckload of shingles delivered to a schoolteacher he didn't like.

His son must have been impressed by his dad's example. He had a truckload of manure delivered to his principal's home.

He was expelled from school.

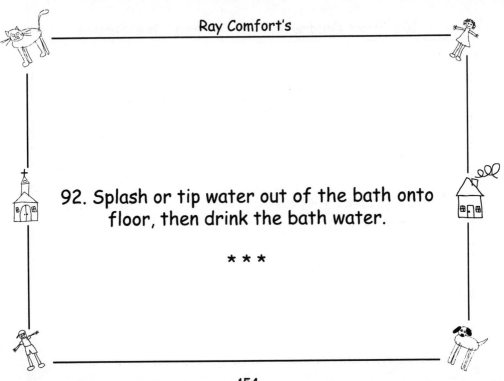

92. Splash or tip water out of the bath onto floor, then drink the bath water.

* * *

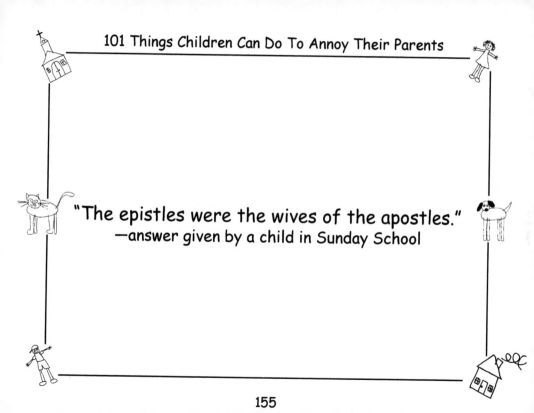

"The epistles were the wives of the apostles."
—answer given by a child in Sunday School

93. Get bored with new (expensive) toys.

A Blank Look

People who deny that there is such a thing as "sin" must never have had children. Kids naturally know how to be selfish.

One of my boys spent what seemed like 30 minutes staring at the wall as he did his homework. Finally I asked him why he had a blank sheet of paper in front of him for such a long time. He then told me that his homework assignment was to write down three kind things he had done for another person.

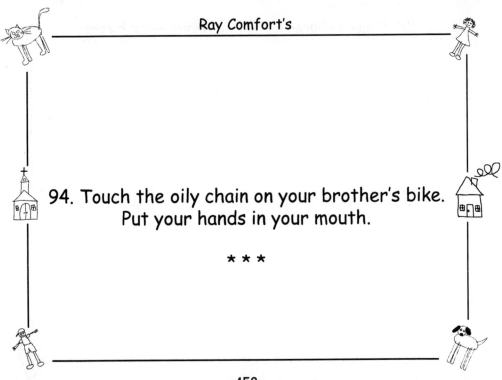

94. Touch the oily chain on your brother's bike.
Put your hands in your mouth.

* * *

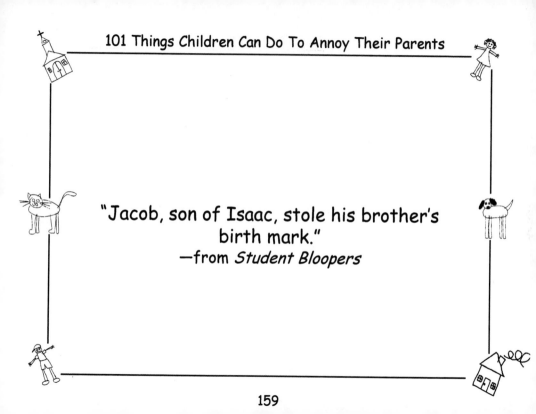

"Jacob, son of Isaac, stole his brother's birth mark."
—from *Student Bloopers*

95. Open kitchen cupboards and hit pot lids together (hard). Smile.

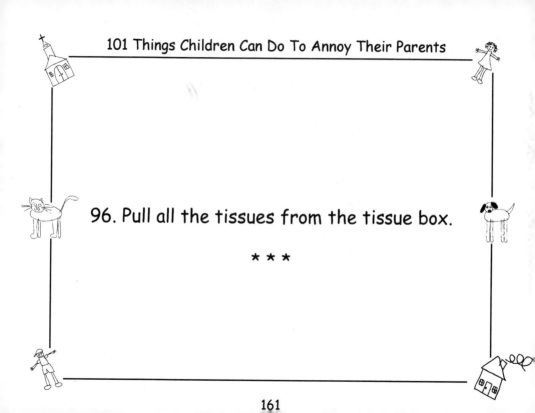

96. Pull all the tissues from the tissue box.

* * *

97. Tip food over the edge of the high chair and watch it hit the floor.

98. Look the other way when a camera is
pointed at you (never smile).

* * *

99. Look cute and innocent when other people see you.

* * *

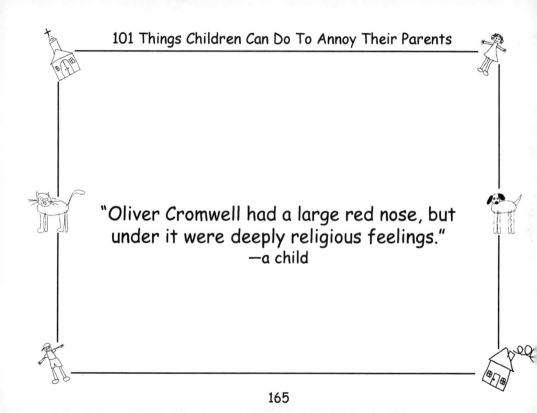

"Oliver Cromwell had a large red nose, but
under it were deeply religious feelings."
—a child

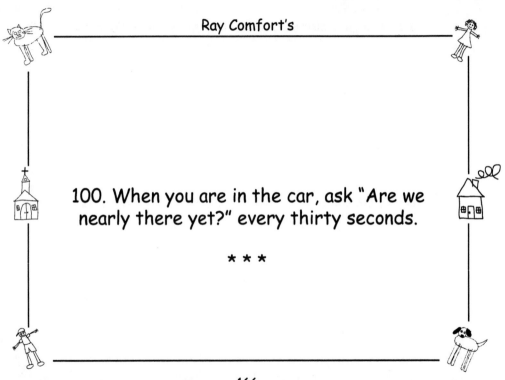

100. When you are in the car, ask "Are we nearly there yet?" every thirty seconds.

* * *

"Daddy, before you married Mommy, who told you how to drive?"
—a child

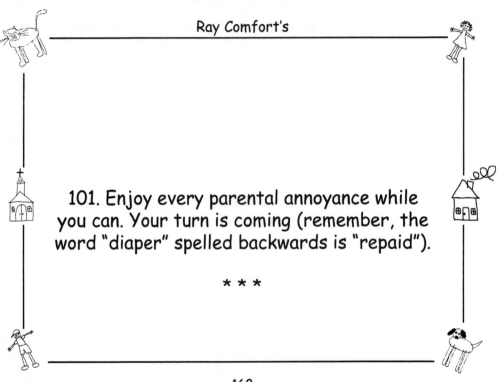

101. Enjoy every parental annoyance while you can. Your turn is coming (remember, the word "diaper" spelled backwards is "repaid").

* * *

"Few things are more satisfying than seeing your own children have teenagers of their own."
—Doug Larson

What About Green?

I was having a shower, when I heard a familiar "Dad . . ." from outside the bathroom door. On inquiry, I found out that my seven-year-old daughter was doing a school project and she had come to me for advice. Few things build a father's esteem like one of his kids coming to him for direction. A father should be a deep well of wisdom, from which a thirsty child may draw.

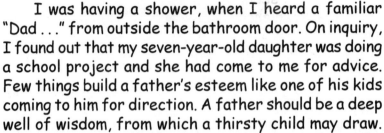

My daughter wanted to know which color to use for her heading on the project. Had she come to the right person! I had spent years in publishing and knew how to catch the eye of the reader. Red was the color she needed. A hot color like red was the ultimate eye-catcher. I called back, "Red is what you should use . . . red on a black background." I smiled as I imagined her eyes widening at my wisdom.

It was then that I heard "What about green?"

Red didn't seem to impress her, so drawing on my years of experience I called back "Yellow. Yellow is what you should use . . . yellow with a black background. The black color throws out the yellow. I suggest yellow."

I heard once again, "What about green?" and called back "Green then . . ." to which I heard, "Thanks Dad!"

The "What about green?" incident reminds me of how we sometimes pray. We know that we should go to God for advice—He is a little wiser than we are, but we have already decided what we want. It is tragic that we have to learn the hard way when it comes to many issues in life.

Sadly, many don't even bother to see what God has to say on a subject, especially when it comes to

raising children. Words like discipline, morality, restraint, virtue, chastity, and self-control, make the world see red. They have green in mind, and they go for it without any reference to the Bible. Then they wonder why they suddenly have a world where kids have kids, kids kill kids, and kids even kill their parents.

The Supreme Court turned on the green light for disaster when it stripped the Ten Commandments from the walls of our schools, but the Commandments fell from the walls of our churches and our homes. When a child is not given God's ten points of view regarding morality, parental honor, respect for life, etc., he will lie, steal and kill without qualms of conscience. Still, not many parents understand why God gave us the Ten Commandments in the first place. They think that they were given as a "standard" by which we are to live.

When we look into the mirror each day, we are simply looking for what damage has been done during the night. When we see ourselves as we are, we then go to the water to wash. The Ten Commandments are simply God's mirror, so that we can see ourselves in truth. Stay with me, because in a moment we will look into the mirror—and it's not a pretty sight.

Many years ago there was a popular hit song called "American Pie." It contained the words: "Did you write the Book of Love, do you have faith in God above, do you believe in rock and roll, can music save your mortal soul?" Then it repeated the words: "This could be the day that I die . . . this could be the day that I die." Sobering, but true. This could be the day that I die. After all, approximately 140,000 people will die in the next 24 hours. The biblical explanation as to why each of us will die is that we have broken God's Law. Just

173

as we suffer the consequences of breaking the law of gravity if we step off a six-story building, so we will suffer the consequences of transgressing God's Moral Law.

Let's now look into the mirror and see if we have broken this Law—the Ten Commandments:

1. Is God first in your life? Do you love Him with all of your heart, mind, soul, and strength? Do you love your neighbor as yourself? Does your love for your family seem like hatred compared to the love you have for the One who gave those loved ones to you?

2. Have you made a god in your own image, to suit yourself?

3. Have you ever used God's holy name in vain, substituting it for a four-lettered filth word to express disgust?

4. Have you kept the Sabbath holy?

5. Have you always honored your parents?

6. Have you hated anyone? Then the Bible says you are a murderer.

7. Have you had sex before marriage? Then you cannot enter God's kingdom. Or have you lusted after another person? The Bible warns that you have committed adultery in your heart.

8. Have you ever stolen something? Then you are a thief.

9. If you have told even one lie, you are a liar, and cannot enter the Kingdom of God.

Finally, have you ever desired something that belonged to someone else? Then you have broken the Tenth Commandment.

Listen to your conscience. Don't look away from the mirror. The Law leaves us all sinners in God's sight.

On Judgment Day we will be found guilty, and end up in Hell forever. A well-known (but dead) politician once said, "Moderation in the pursuit of justice is no virtue." God is utterly virtuous. He will pursue justice right down to the thoughts of our hearts.

Perhaps you are sorry for your sins, and you even confess them to God. But that doesn't mean that He will forgive you-no matter how sincere you are. Let me explain why. Imagine you are standing guilty in front of a judge. You face a $50,000 fine, and say, "Judge, I'm truly sorry for my crime." He would probably say, "So you should be! Now are you able to pay the $50,000 fine or not?" A judge must have grounds upon which he can release you. If I paid your fine, then you would be free from the demands of the law. That's precisely what God did in the person of Jesus Christ. Each of us stand guilty of breaking God's Law, but because

Jesus paid our fine on the cross 2,000 years ago, God can forgive us on the grounds of His suffering death. That's why you need Jesus Christ as your Savior. Without Him, the Law will send you to Hell, and you will have no one to blame but yourself. God will make sure justice is carried out. The Bible says, "God commended His love towards us, in that, while we were yet sinners, Christ died for us." He gave His sinless life on the cross, showing the depth of God's love for us. We broke God's Law—He paid the fine so that we could be free from its perfect demands. Then He rose from the dead, and defeated the power of the grave.

If you repent, trust in the Savior and obey His word, God will forgive your sins and grant you everlasting life. The Bible says that all humanity is held captive to the fear of, and power of death (Hebrews 2:15). If you don't face your fear of death,

then you will run from it until the day you die—and that day will come. The proof of your sin will be your death.

Today, not only face the reality that you will die, but do something about it—obey the Gospel and live. Please, for your sake and for the sake of your children, confess your sins to God, put your faith in Jesus Christ, then read the Bible daily and obey what you read. God will never let you down.

Thank you for taking the time to read this book. May God bless you and keep you and your family in health.

For a complete list of books, tracts, tapes and videos by Ray Comfort call 1(800) 437-1893 or see www.raycomfort.com

or write to:
Living Waters Publications
P. O. Box 1172
Bellflower, CA 90706